# LOU GEHRIG

## THE LUCKIEST MAN

David A. Adler

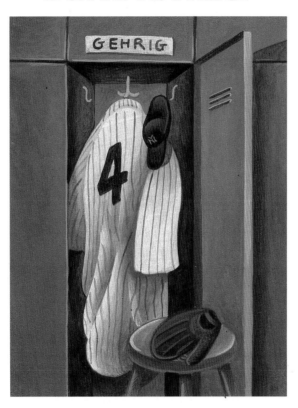

ILLUSTRATED BY

Terry Widener

VOYAGER BOOKS     HARCOURT, INC.     *San Diego*   *New York*   *London* www.harcourt.com

First Voyager Books edition 2001
Voyager Books is a trademark of Harcourt, Inc., registered in the United States of America and other jurisdictions.

The Library of Congress has cataloged the hardcover edition as follows:
Adler, David A.
Lou Gehrig: the luckiest man/David A. Adler; illustrated by Terry Widener.
p.    cm.
Summary: Traces the life of the Yankees' star ballplayer, focusing on his character and his struggle with the terminal disease amyotrophic lateral sclerosis.
1. Gehrig, Lou, 1903–1941—Juvenile literature.    2. Baseball players—United States—Biography—Juvenile literature.    (1. Gehrig, Lou, 1903–1941.
2. Baseball players.)    I. Widener, Terry, ill.    II. Title.
GV865.G4A35    1997
796.357'092—dc20
(B)      95-7997
ISBN 0-15-200523-4
ISBN 0-15-202483-2 pb

H G F E D C B A

The illustrations in this book were done in Golden acrylics on Strathmore Bristol board.
The display type was set in Radiant and Copperplate Gothic.
The text type was set in Benguiat Book.
Color separations by Bright Arts, Ltd., Singapore
Printed and bound by Tien Wah Press, Singapore
This book was printed on Arctic matte paper.
Production supervision by Sandra Grebenar and Ginger Boyer
Designed by Camilla Filancia

*I would like to thank Hollee Haswell, curator of the Columbiana Collection, for her help in researching the Columbia University image.*

*—T. W.*

A NOTE ABOUT THE YANKEE UNIFORM

*During the fourteen years, from 1925 to 1939, that Lou Gehrig played with the New York Yankees, the uniforms for home and away games changed numerous times. The Yankees began putting numbers (indicating players' batting order) on the backs of the jerseys in 1929—a precedent that became major-league standard by 1932. The NY monogram (which had sporadically been used in the early years of this century) reappeared in 1936 on the front of the home game jerseys. In 1939 all sixteen major-league teams, including the Yankees, wore a patch on the upper left sleeve to commemorate the centennial year of the game's invention.*

*For* PHIL RIZZUTO, *whose sure hands and kind heart have brought joy to several generations of New Yorkers, and for* MICHAEL SETH ADLER, *one of his greatest fans*
　　　　　—D. A. A.

*For my wife,* LESLIE; *our children,* KATE, KELLEE, *and* MICHAEL; *and* MICHÈLE
　　　　　—T. W.

# 1903

was a year of great beginnings. Henry Ford sold his first automobile and the Wright Brothers made the first successful flight in an airplane. In baseball, the first World Series was played. The team later known as the Yankees moved from Baltimore to New York. And on June 19, 1903, Henry Louis Gehrig was born. He would become one of the greatest players in baseball history.

Lou Gehrig was born in the Yorkville section of New York City. It was an area populated with poor immigrants like his parents, Heinrich and Christina Gehrig, who had come to the United States from Germany.

Christina Gehrig had great hopes for her son Lou. She dreamed that he would attend college and become an accountant or an engineer. She insisted that he study hard. Through eight years of grade school, Lou didn't miss a single day.

Lou's mother thought games and sports were a waste of time. But Lou loved sports. He got up early to play the games he loved—baseball, soccer, and football. He played until it was time to go to school. In high school Lou was a star on his school's baseball team.

After high school Lou Gehrig went to Columbia University. He was on the base-ball team there, too, and on April 26, 1923, a scout for the New York Yankees watched him play. Lou hit two long home runs in that game. Soon after that he was signed to play for the Yankees.

The Yankees offered Lou a $1,500 bonus to sign plus a good salary. His family needed the money. Lou quit college and joined the Yankees. Lou's mother was furious. She was convinced that he was ruining his life.

On June 1, 1925, the Yankee manager sent Lou to bat for the shortstop. The next day Lou played in place of first baseman Wally Pipp. Those were the first two games in what would become an amazing record: For the next fourteen years Lou Gehrig played in 2,130 consecutive Yankee games. The boy who never missed a day of grade school became a man who never missed a game.

Lou Gehrig played despite stomachaches, fevers, a sore arm, back pains, and broken fingers. Lou's constant play earned him the nickname Iron Horse. All he would say about his amazing record was, "That's the way I am."

Lou was shy and modest, but people who watched him knew

just how good he was. In 1927 Lou's teammate Babe Ruth hit sixty home runs, the most hit up to that time in one season. But it was Lou Gehrig who was selected that year by the baseball writers as the American League's Most Valuable Player. He was selected again as the league's MVP in 1936.

Then, during the 1938 baseball season—and for no apparent reason—Lou Gehrig stopped hitting. One newspaper reported that Lou was swinging as hard as he could, but when he hit the ball it didn't go anywhere.

Lou exercised. He took extra batting practice. He even tried changing the way he stood and held his bat. He worked hard during the winter of 1938 and watched his diet.

But the following spring Lou's playing was worse. Time after time he swung at the ball and missed. He had trouble fielding. And he even had problems off the field. In the clubhouse he fell down while he was getting dressed.

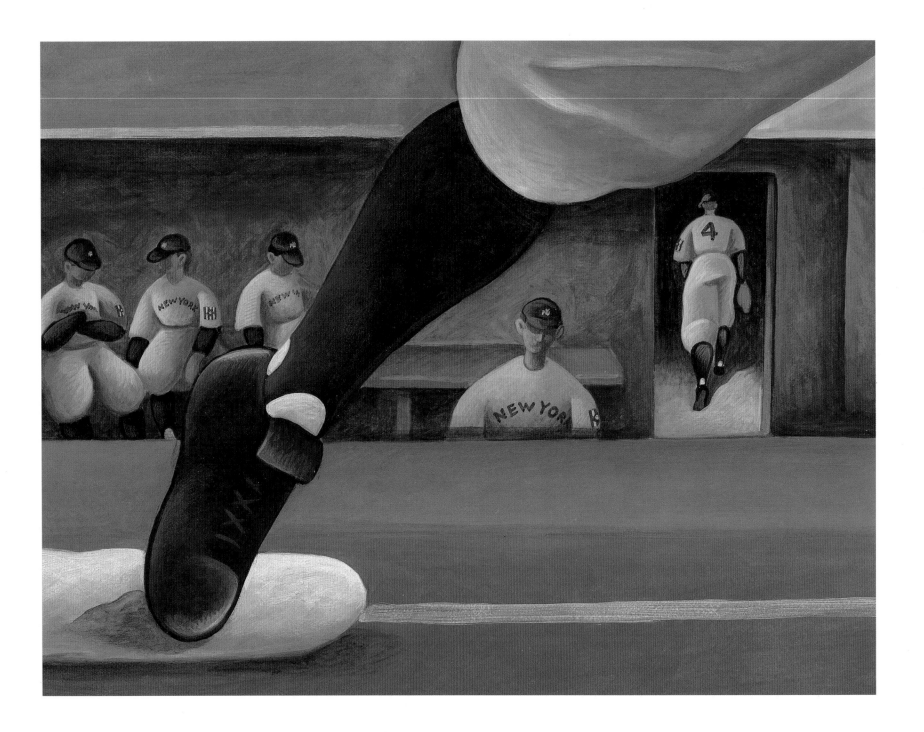

Some people said Yankee manager Joe McCarthy should take Lou out of the lineup. But McCarthy refused. He had great respect for Lou and said, "Gehrig plays as long as he wants to play." But Lou wasn't selfish. On May 2, 1939, he told Joe McCarthy, "I'm benching my-self...for the good of the team."

When reporters asked why he took himself out, Lou didn't say he felt weak or how hard it was for him to run. Lou made no excuses. He just said that he couldn't hit and he couldn't field.

On June 13, 1939, Lou went to the Mayo Clinic in Rochester, Minnesota, to be examined by specialists. On June 19, his thirty-sixth birthday, they told Lou's wife, Eleanor, what was wrong. He was suffering from amyotrophic lateral sclerosis, a deadly disease that affects the central nervous system.

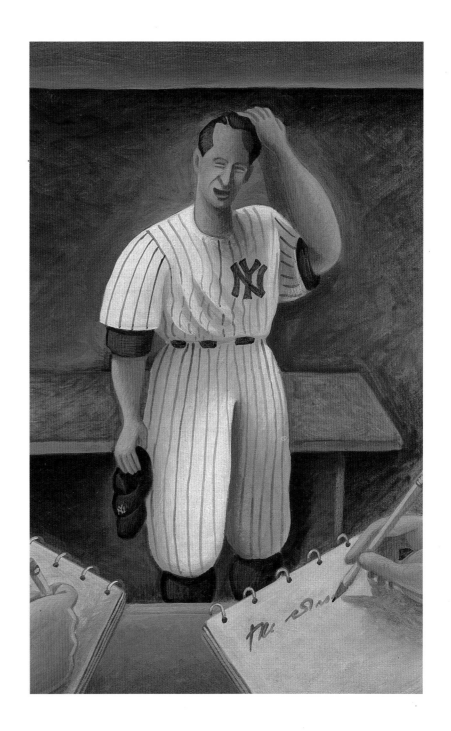

Lou stayed with the team, but he didn't play. He was losing weight. His hair was turning gray. He didn't have to be told he was dying. He knew it. "I don't have long to go," he told a teammate.

Lou loved going to the games, being in the clubhouse, and sitting with his teammates. Before each game Lou brought the Yankee lineup card to the umpire at home plate. A teammate or coach walked with him, to make sure he didn't fall. Whenever Lou came onto the field the fans stood up and cheered for brave Lou Gehrig.

But Yankee fans and the team wanted to do more. They wanted Lou to know how deeply they felt about him. So they made July 4, 1939, Lou Gehrig Appreciation Day at Yankee Stadium.

Many of the players from the 1927 Yankees—perhaps the best baseball team ever—came to honor their former teammate. There was a marching band and gifts. Many people spoke, too. Fiorello La Guardia, the mayor of New York City, told Lou, "You are the greatest prototype of good sportsmanship and citizenship."

When the time came for Lou to thank everyone, he was too moved to speak. But the fans wanted to hear him and chanted, "We want Gehrig! We want Gehrig!"

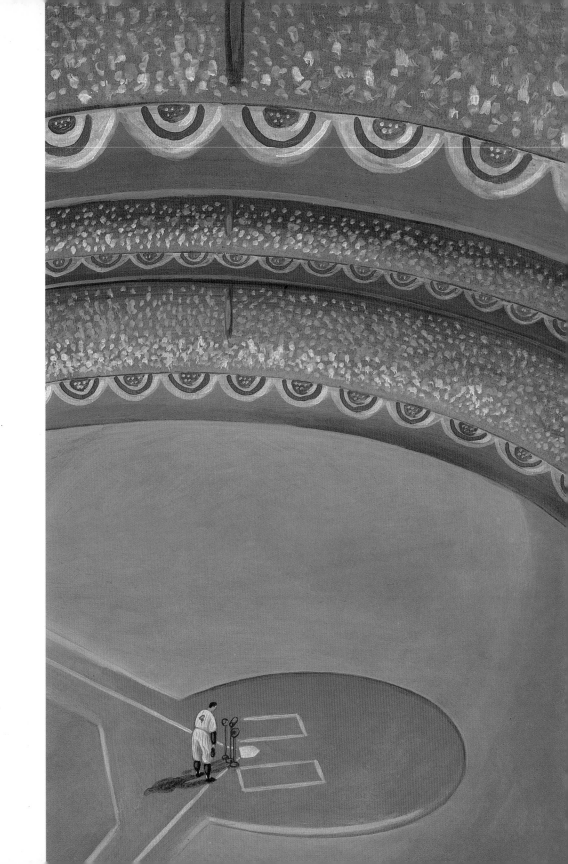

Dressed in his Yankee uniform, Lou Gehrig walked slowly to the array of microphones. He wiped his eyes, and with his baseball cap in his hands, his head down, he slowly spoke.

"Fans," he said, "for the past two weeks you have been reading about a bad break I got. Yet today I consider myself the luckiest man on the face of the earth."

It was a courageous speech. Lou didn't complain about his terrible illness. Instead he spoke of his many blessings and of the future. "Sure, I'm lucky," he said when he spoke of his years in baseball. "Sure, I'm lucky," he said again when he spoke of his fans and family.

Lou spoke about how good people had been to him. He praised his teammates. He thanked his parents and his wife, whom he called a tower of strength.

The more than sixty thousand fans in Yankee Stadium stood to honor Lou Gehrig. His last words to them—and to the many thousands more sitting by their radios and listening—were, "So I close in saying that I might have had a bad break, but I have an awful lot to live for. Thank you."

Lou stepped back from the microphones and wiped his eyes. The stadium crowd let out a tremendous roar, and Babe Ruth did what many people must have wanted to do that day. He threw his arms around Lou Gehrig and gave him a great warm hug.

The band played the song "I Love You Truly," and the fans chanted, "We love you, Lou."

When Lou Gehrig left the stadium later that afternoon, he told a teammate, "I'm going to remember this day for a long time."

In December 1939 Lou Gehrig was voted into the Baseball Hall of Fame. And the Yankees retired his uniform. No one else on the team would ever wear the number four. It was the first time a major-league baseball team did that to honor one of its players.

Mayor Fiorello La Guardia thought Lou's courage might inspire some of the city's troubled youths to be courageous, too. He offered Lou a job working with former prisoners as a member of the New York City Parole Commission. Lou had many opportunities to earn more money, but he believed this job would enable him to do something for the city that had given him so much.

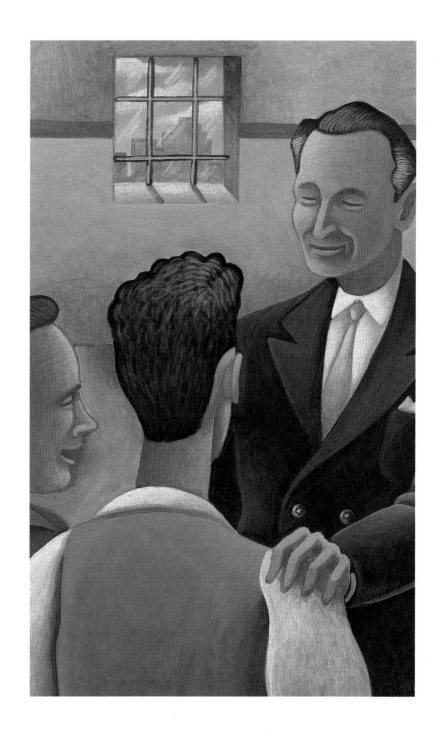

Within little more than a year, Lou had to leave his job. He was too weak to keep working. He stayed at home, unable to do the simplest task.

Lou had many visitors. He didn't speak to them of his illness or of dying. When he saw one friend visibly upset by the way he looked, Lou told him not to worry. "I'll gradually get better," he said. In cards to his friends Lou wrote, "We have much to be thankful for."

By the middle of May 1941, Lou hardly left his bed. Then on Monday, June 2, 1941, just after ten o'clock at night, Lou Gehrig died. He was thirty-seven years old.

On June 4 the Yankee game was canceled because of rain. Some people thought it was fitting that the Yankees did not play; this was the day of Lou Gehrig's funeral.

At the funeral the minister announced that there would be no speeches. "We need none," he said, "because you all knew him." That seemed fitting, too, for modest Lou Gehrig.